S. Hrg. 114–750

INTERNATIONAL CYBERSECURITY STRATEGY: DETERRING FOREIGN THREATS AND BUILDING GLOBAL CYBER NORMS

HEARING

BEFORE THE

SUBCOMMITTEE ON EAST ASIA, THE PACIFIC, AND INTERNATIONAL CYBER SECURITY POLICY

OF THE

COMMITTEE ON FOREIGN RELATIONS UNITED STATES SENATE

ONE HUNDRED FOURTEENTH CONGRESS

SECOND SESSION

———

MAY 25, 2016

———

Printed for the use of the Committee on Foreign Relations

Available via the World Wide Web:
http://www.govinfo.gov

U.S. GOVERNMENT PUBLISHING OFFICE

28–853 PDF   WASHINGTON : 2018

CONTENTS

(III)

INTERNATIONAL CYBERSECURITY STRATEGY: DETERRING FOREIGN THREATS AND BUILDING GLOBAL CYBER NORMS

WEDNESDAY, MAY 25, 2016

U.S. SENATE,
SUBCOMMITTEE ON EAST ASIA, THE PACIFIC, AND
INTERNATIONAL CYBERSECURITY POLICY
COMMITTEE ON FOREIGN RELATIONS,
Washington, DC.

The subcommittee met, pursuant to notice, at 10:05 a.m. in Room SD–419, Dirksen Senate Office Building, Hon. Cory Gardner, chairman of the subcommittee, presiding.

Present: Senators Gardner [presiding] and Cardin.

OPENING STATEMENT OF HON. CORY GARDNER, U.S. SENATOR FROM COLORADO

Senator GARDNER. This hearing will come to order.

Let me welcome you all to the sixth hearing for the Senate Foreign Relations Subcommittee on East Asia, Pacific, and International Cybersecurity Policy in the 114th Congress and our first hearing in 2016.

I want to thank Ranking Member Cardin who, of course, also serves as the ranking member of the full committee, for his cooperation as we continue our important work together to address the important issues within this subcommittee's jurisdiction.

Today's hearing will be our second hearing on cybersecurity in this subcommittee which I believe goes to show the extent to which cyber issues has become a strategic matter, critical to the foreign policy of our Nation and subsequently to this committee's work.

And we are glad to welcome back our witness the State Department's cybersecurity coordinator, Chris Painter. This is your second time I believe testifying before this subcommittee. We hope to hear from Mr. Painter today about what has changed since we met just over a year ago at our first cyber hearing of this subcommittee, what global threats we are still facing, and most importantly, what we can do as a Nation to deter those threats.

The State Department has now released the Department of State International Cyberspace Policy Strategy, as mandated by the amendment Senator Cardin and I authored to the 2016 omnibus legislation. We thank Mr. Painter for fulfilling this congressional mandate and producing this document which will better inform this committee's efforts going forward. And I commend you for standing up the cyber efforts at State and elevating cyber issues to the forefront of our Nation's diplomacy.

But we still, obviously, have a lot of questions about how this approach is being implemented, how effective it is in deterring foreign cyber threats, and how we can continue to build viable norms in cyberspace. Our efforts include deterring China and Chinese actors from continuing to conduct commercial espionage against the United States with agreements made last fall, how those agreements are or are not being implemented. The questions remain about sensitive data being stolen in the breach of the Office of Personnel Management last year and other circumstances around the globe.

And so as we discuss Russia and we discuss Ukraine and we discuss Iran, we discuss United Nations activities, this is an important hearing to place our cyber policy in the strategic realm.

And so with that, I am going to just let everybody know right now we are anticipating votes at 11:00 o'clock, and so we will wait as long as we can, if necessary, into that vote series before we adjourn the committee hearing.

So thank you, Mr. Painter.

And with that, I will turn it to our ranking member, Senator Cardin from Maryland.

STATEMENT OF HON. BENJAMIN L. CARDIN, U.S. SENATOR FROM MARYLAND

Senator CARDIN. Well, Senator Gardner, first of all, thank you for your leadership on this subcommittee. It is a critically important subcommittee that deals with East Asia, deals with the Pacific, and deals with international cybersecurity policy. We certainly have had a very busy agenda under your leadership, and it has been a pleasure to work with you.

We should note the President is in Vietnam. Part of our challenge is the development of stronger ties with the countries of Asia. We have also, of course, been very much engaged in North Korea and their proliferation activities, as well as of course China.

And then later today, there will be a full committee briefing on the Trafficking in Persons Report, and there are several countries in Asia that are of major interest in regards to trafficking and other human rights concerns.

So this has been a very busy subcommittee and I thank you for the manner that we have been able to work together, as we should, on foreign policy issues without partisan division. So thank you very much.

Cyber represents a new domain in global affairs likely to be significant in shaping the 21st century as nuclear weapons were in shaping the 20th century. How the United States and others in the international community develop norms of behavior, assure freedom of expression, and understand how concepts such as deterrence, supply, and cyberspace will be critical foreign policy challenges in the years ahead.

These are not going to be easy because what one person sees as a national security issue, another looks at as repressive to the ability of individuals to be able to get information in their country. How cyber technology is used to advance the flow of information and to protect us against cyber attacks can also be used to repress people from being able to get information by governments that look at cyber as a threat to their totalitarian regimes.

So we have challenges here, and how we deal with this is going to be one of the major security challenges to face America. The Internet must belong to its users, not just the states. There are especially repressive regimes like Russia and China that are seeking to block or control access to their people to the Internet. We will not be able to realize the full potential of the Internet to support freedom, civil society, and human dignity as long as certain nations continue to severely restrict Internet freedom. We need to be cognizant of the dangers that cyberspace presents for human progress and political rights. The same tools of Internet freedom that can be used to organize movements for free speech can also be used by ISIS to spew hatred and incite violence against the innocents.

Technologies with the potential to open up access to governments can also be hijacked to crush dissent and crush human rights. New technologies do not take sides in the struggle for human rights, but the United States must. We need to be leaders in upholding the principles of Internet freedom and human rights in cyberspace. We need to synchronize America's undisputed technology leadership with indisputable values and principles. That is what America brings to this international debate, and that is why it is critically important that we develop acceptable international norms in regards to the use of cyber and what is expected.

So, obviously, we look forward to building those norms. Last year, the United States and China reached an unprecedented deal to combat cyber-enabled theft of intellectual property with the intent of providing competitive advantages to companies or commercial sectors. To me that was an incredibly important moment, but how is it being implemented? And how will that lead to acceptable international norms?

The agreement took a new significance at the G20 summit in Turkey when China agreed to join the rest of the G20 nations and jointly affirming for the first time that no country should conduct or support information or communication technology-enabled theft of intellectual property with the intent of providing competitive advantages to companies or commercial sectors.

I will support the U.S.-China cyber agreement. I am concerned that China may not be living up to its terms, and I hope today that we will have a chance to review that.

I am concerned that there is too much ambiguity in our current cyber deterrence policy, which leaves our adversaries confused about what behavior in cyberspace the United States is willing to tolerate. We have what we have learned from the Sony attack and the OPM hack in determining what is considered appropriate in terms of an attack as opposed to mapping or other acceptable activities. What have we learned? Where do you draw the right line, and is that clear by U.S. policies internationally?

Mr. Chairman, there are a lot of issues that we need to review, and this subcommittee has the responsibility to continue our active engagement and we are doing that today by this hearing. And I thank you, and I look forward to listening to Mr. Painter.

Senator GARDNER. Thank you, Senator Cardin.

And, of course, we will turn to our witness, Chris Painter, today, the Honorable Chris Painter who serves as the State Department's Coordinator for Cyber Issues. In this capacity, Mr. Painter coordinates and leads the United States' diplomatic efforts to implement the President's international strategy for cyberspace. He works closely with components across the Department, other agencies, the White House, the private sector, and civil society.

Prior to joining the State Department, Mr. Painter served in the White House as Senior Director for Cybersecurity Policy on the National Security staff. During his 2 years at the White House, Mr. Painter was a senior member of the team that conducted the President's cyberspace policy review and subsequently served as Acting Cybersecurity Coordinator. He coordinated the development of the President's 2011 international strategy for cyberspace.

Welcome again, Mr. Painter, to the subcommittee, and thank you for your service. We look forward to your testimony.

STATEMENT OF CHRISTOPHER PAINTER, COORDINATOR FOR CYBER ISSUES, U.S. DEPARTMENT OF STATE, WASHINGTON, DC

Mr. PAINTER. Thank you very much. Chairman Gardner, Ranking Member Gardner, members of the Subcommittee on East Asia, the Pacific, and International Cybersecurity Policy, it is indeed a pleasure to appear again before your subcommittee to provide an update on our efforts to deter foreign threats and promote global norms in cyberspace. I would agree that the fact that this committee has shown attention to this issue helps heighten this issue as a foreign policy issue both here and around the world.

Since I testified before your subcommittee 1 year ago, the Department of State has continued to make significant progress working closely with other Federal Departments and agencies across all of our policy priorities, including international security, Internet governance, cybersecurity due diligence, cyber crime, Internet freedom, and Internet access.

And it is also important to note, as the chairman noted, that last month, the Department submitted to Congress the Department of State International Cyberspace Policy Strategy, and therefore today I am going to focus my remarks on a few of our recent successes in promoting our framework for international cyber stability. However, I am happy to answer any questions regarding the strategy which addresses all of our priorities in greater detail or any questions from my written testimony that was submitted for the record.

As described in those documents, we have spearheaded the promotion of a framework for stability in cyberspace based on, first, the applicability of international law to state behavior in cyberspace; second, the identification of additional voluntary norms of responsible state behavior in cyberspace that apply during peacetime; and third, the development and implementation of practical confidence building measures to reduce the risk of misperception and escalation.

I would like to highlight today some significant developments that have occurred in the last year to advance this framework.

Of special interest to this subcommittee are developments with China. As the subcommittee is well aware, the United States strongly opposes the use of cyber technology to steal intellectual property for commercial advantage and has continuously raised this concern with China for some time. In September 2015, the U.S. and China reached agreement during President Xi Jinping's state visit on several key commitments on cyber issues. Among those commitments, in addition to the ones relating to law enforcement cooperation, were that, one, neither country's government will conduct or knowingly support cyber-enabled theft of intellectual property for commercial advantage and, two, both governments will work together to further identify and promote appropriate norms of state behavior in cyberspace and hold a senior experts group on international security issues in cyberspace.

While these commitments do not resolve all of our challenges with China on cyber issues, nevertheless they do represent a step forward in our efforts to address one of the sharpest areas of disagreement in the U.S.-China bilateral relationship.

I would also note that 2 weeks ago today on May 11th, we hosted the first meeting of the senior experts group in Washington on international security issues in cyberspace, which provided a forum to further engage China on its views and seek common ground regarding norms of state behavior in cyberspace and other topics.

The agreement with China last year is in part built upon the success we had a few months earlier when the United Nations Group of Governmental Experts reached a consensus on its third report since 2009 on issues related to international security in cyberspace.

The 2015 GGE report's most significant achievement was its recommendation regarding voluntary norms of state behavior designed for peacetime, which included concepts that have been championed by the U.S. This included norms against harming critical infrastructure, our computer security incident response teams, as well as the norm that states respond to appropriate requests in mitigating malicious cyber activity emanating from their territory.

Both of these developments that I just mentioned fed into a third major accomplishment. Last November, the leaders of the G20 meeting in Turkey strongly endorsed the U.S. approach to promoting stability in cyberspace. The leaders' communique affirmed that states should not conduct or support cyber theft of intellectual property for commercial advantage. The communique also highlighted the 2015 GGE report I discussed, affirmed international law and, in particular, the U.N. charter applies to state conduct in cyberspace, and endorsed the view that all states should abide by norms of responsible state behavior in cyberspace.

These three developments occurring in a remarkably short period of time, along with recent agreements in two regional security organizations to advance our work in developing cyber confidence building measures, collectively represents a major step towards international acceptance of the U.S. approach to promoting stability in cyberspace. It gives us great momentum as we work to convince more states to endorse our approach at the leaders' level as we move into the upcoming round of the GGE that begins in August where we hope to further develop this framework.

While we can be proud of our recent successes, it is important to also acknowledge that we still face a range of policy and technical challenges to our vision of an open, interoperable, secure, and reliable cyberspace.

As we look ahead, cybersecurity will continue to be a challenge for the United States when we take into consideration the rapidly expanding environment of global cyber threats, the increasing reliance on information, the reality that many developing nations are still in the early stages of their cyber maturity, and the ongoing and increasingly sophisticated use of information technology by terrorists and other criminals. Therefore, the Department of State anticipates a continued increase and an expansion of our cyber-focused diplomatic and capacity building efforts for the foreseeable future.

Again, I am happy to be here before the subcommittee and happy to take any questions.

[Mr. Painter's prepared statement follows:]

PREPARED STATEMENT OF CHRISTOPHER M. E. PAINTER

Chairman Gardner, Ranking Member Cardin, members of the Subcommittee on East Asia, the Pacific, and International Cybersecurity Policy, it is a pleasure to appear again before your Subcommittee to provide an update on key developments in our cyber foreign policy efforts.

Since I testified before your Subcommittee one year ago, the Department of State (the Department) has continued to work closely with other Federal departments and agencies and has made significant progress in a number of areas.

It is also important to note that last month, as required by the Consolidated Appropriations Act for 2016, the Department submitted to Congress the Department of State International Cyberspace Policy Strategy (the Strategy) that included a report on the Department's work to implement the President's 2011 International Strategy for Cyberspace, as well as a discussion of our efforts to promote norms of responsible state behavior in cyberspace, alternative concepts for norms promoted by certain other countries, threats facing the United States, tools available to the President to deter malicious actors, and resources required to build international norms. I appreciate the opportunity today to provide an update on our progress as well as the challenges we face in a number of areas.

As reflected in the Strategy we provided to Congress last month, the Department of State structures its cyberspace diplomacy in close cooperation with our interagency partners—including the Departments of Justice, Commerce, Defense, Homeland Security, and Treasury, and the Intelligence Community—around the following interrelated, dynamic, and cross-cutting policy pillars drawn from the President's International Strategy for Cyberspace: digital economy; international security; promoting cybersecurity due diligence; combating cybercrime; Internet governance; Internet freedom; and international development and capacity building, as well as cross-cutting issues such as countering the use of the Internet for terrorist purposes. In addition, as we noted, the Department actively is mainstreaming cyberspace issues into its foreign diplomatic engagements and building the necessary internal capacity.

I am happy to answer any questions regarding the Strategy, which discusses all of these policy priorities in greater detail, including specific accomplishments from our robust bilateral and multilateral diplomatic engagements and highlights from the roles and contributions of other Federal agencies.

In spite of the successes outlined in the Strategy, the U.S. vision for an open, interoperable, secure, and reliable Internet faces a range of policy and technical challenges. Many of these challenges were described in my testimony last year, and they largely remain. I would like to focus my time today delving specifically into our efforts to promote a broad international framework for cyber stability, as well some of the alternative views regarding the Internet that some governments are promoting. I will also spend some time discussing the technical challenges and threats posed by continuing malicious cyber activity directed at the United States, as well as our allies, and the tools we have at our disposal to deter these actions.

DIPLOMATIC EFFORTS TO SHAPE THE POLICY ENVIRONMENT

BUILDING A FRAMEWORK FOR INTERNATIONAL STABILITY IN CYBERSPACE

The Department of State, working with our interagency partners, is guided by the vision of the President's International Strategy for Cyberspace, which is to promote a strategic framework of international cyber stability designed to achieve and maintain a peaceful cyberspace environment where all states are able to fully realize its benefits, where there are advantages to cooperating against common threats and avoiding conflict, and where there is little incentive for states to engage in disruptive behavior or to attack one another.

This framework has three key elements: (1) global affirmation that international law applies to state behavior in cyberspace; (2) development of an international consensus on and promotion of additional voluntary norms of responsible state behavior in cyberspace that apply during peacetime; and (3) development and implementation of practical confidence building measures (CBMs), which promote stability in cyberspace by reducing the risks of misperception and escalation.

Since 2009, the United Nations Group of Governmental Experts on Developments in the Field of Information and Telecommunications in the Context of International Security (UN GGE) has served as a productive and groundbreaking expert-level venue for the United States to build support for this framework. The consensus recommendations of the three UN GGE reports in 2010, 2013, and 2015 have set the standard for the international community on international cyberspace norms and CBMs. The UN GGE process will continue to play a central role in our efforts to fully promulgate this framework when it reconvenes in August 2016.

Applicability of international law. The first and most fundamental pillar of our framework for international cyber stability is the applicability of existing international law to state behavior in cyberspace. The 2013 UN GGE report was a landmark achievement that affirmed the applicability of existing international law, including the UN Charter, to state conduct in cyberspace. The 2013 report underscored that states must act in cyberspace under the established international obligations and commitments that have guided their actions for decades—in peacetime and during conflict—and states must meet their international obligations regarding internationally wrongful acts attributable to them. The 2014-2015 UN GGE also made progress on issues related to international law by affirming the applicability of the inherent right to self-defense as recognized in Article 51 of the UN Charter, and noting the law of armed conflict's fundamental principles of humanity, necessity, proportionality, and distinction.

Norms of responsible state behavior. The United States is also building consensus on a set of additional, voluntary norms of responsible state behavior in cyberspace that define key areas of risk that would be of national and/or economic security concern to all states and which should be off-limits during times of peace. If observed, these stability measures—which are measures of self-restraint—can contribute substantially to conflict prevention and stability. The United States was the first state to propose a set of specific peacetime cyber norms, including the cybersecurity of critical infrastructure, the protection of computer security incident response teams (CSIRTs), and cooperation between states in responding to appropriate requests in mitigating malicious cyber activity emanating from their territory. In May 2015, Secretary of State Kerry highlighted these norms in his speech in Seoul, South Korea, on an open and secure Internet. The 2015 UN GGE report's most significant achievement was its recommendation for voluntary norms of state behavior designed for peacetime, which included concepts championed by the United States.

Confidence Building Measures. Together with our work on law and voluntary norms, cyber CBMs have the potential to contribute substantially to international cyber stability. CBMs have been used for decades to build confidence, reduce risk, and increase transparency in other areas of international concern. Examples of cyber CBMs include: transparency measures, such as sharing national strategies or doctrine; cooperative measures, such as an initiative to combat a particular cyber incident or threat actor; and stability measures, such as committing to refrain from a certain activity of concern. Cyber CBMs are being developed, and are in the first stages of implementation, in two regional venues—the Organization for Security and Cooperation in Europe (OSCE) and the ASEAN Regional Forum where agreement was reached in 2015 on a detailed work plan with a proposed set of CBMs for future implementation.

Although many of the elements of the framework I have described above may seem selfevident to an American audience, it is important to recognize that cyber issues are new to many states, and as I describe later in my testimony, there are also many states that hold alternative views on how we should promote cyber stability. Notwithstanding these headwinds, as well as the fact that diplomatic negotiations on other issues can take many years, if not decades, the United States and its allies have made substantial progress in recent years towards advancing our strategic framework of international cyber stability. At this point, I would like to highlight examples from last year that reflect our progress.

U.S.-China Cyber Commitments

The United States strongly opposes the use of cyber technology to steal intellectual property for commercial advantage, and has raised this concern with Chinese interlocutors for several years. In 2014, the U.S. indicted five members of the Chinese military for hacking, economic espionage, and other offenses directed at six U.S. entities. This led China to suspend the U.S.-China Cyber Working Group. The U.S. and China, however, reached agreement during President Xi Jinping's state visit in September 2015 on several key commitments on cyber issues. These commitments are:

1. both governments agreed to cooperate and provide timely responses to requests for information and assistance regarding malicious cyber activity emanating from their territories;
2. neither country's government will conduct or knowingly support cyber-enabled theft of intellectual property for commercial advantage;
3. both governments will work together to further identify and promote appropriate norms of state behavior in cyberspace and hold a senior experts group on international security issues in cyberspace; and
4. both governments will establish a Ministerial-level joint dialogue mechanism on fighting cybercrime and related issues.

Two weeks ago today—on May 11—the United States hosted the first meeting of the senior experts group in Washington on international security issues in cyberspace, which provided a forum to further engage China on its views and seek common ground regarding norms of state behavior in cyberspace and other topics. The Department of State led the U.S. delegation that included participation from the Department of Defense and other U.S. government agencies. The senior experts group helps us advance the growing international consensus on international law and voluntary cyber norms of state behavior. We also have encouraged China to join us in pushing for other states to affirm these principles in international forums like the Group of Twenty (G20), and will continue to do so.

To implement other commitments reached during President Xi's visit, the United States and China held the first ministerial level dialogue on cybercrime and other related issues in Washington on December 1, 2015. Attorney General Loretta Lynch and Homeland Security Secretary Jeh Johnson, together with Chinese State Councilor Guo Shengkun, co-chaired the first U.S.-China High-Level Joint Dialogue on Cybercrime and Related Issues to foster mutual understanding and enhance cooperation on law enforcement and network protection issues. The second dialogue is scheduled to occur next month in Beijing, China.

Moreover, regarding the commitment that neither government will conduct or knowingly support cyber-enabled theft for commercial gain, Deputy Secretary of State Blinken testified last month before the full Committee on Foreign Relations that the United States is "watching very closely to ensure this commitment is followed by action."

The outcomes of last year's Xi-Obama summit focus on concrete actions and arrangements that will allow us to hold Beijing accountable to the commitments they have made. These commitments do not resolve all our challenges with China on cyber issues. However, they do represent a step forward in our efforts to address one of the sharpest areas of disagreement in the U.S.-China bilateral relationship.

Group of Twenty (G20) Antalya Summit

In November 2015, the leaders of the G20 met in Antalya, Turkey, to discuss and make progress on a wide range of critical issues facing the global economy. At the conclusion of the Antalya Summit, the strong final communique issued by the G20 leaders affirmed the U.S.-championed vision of international cyber stability and its pillars.

Among other things, the G20 leaders affirmed in their statement that "no country should conduct or support the ICT-enabled theft of intellectual property, including trade secrets or other confidential business information, with the intent of providing competitive advantages to companies or commercial sectors." They also highlighted the "key role played by the United Nations in developing norms" and the work of the UN GGE and its 2015 report. Addressing our overall framework, the G20 leaders stated that they "affirm that international law, and in particular the UN Charter, is applicable to state conduct in the use of ICTs and commit ourselves to the view that all states should abide by norms of responsible state behavior in the use of ICTs . . . "

The G20 leaders' communique represents a remarkable endorsement of our approach to promoting stability in cyberspace. But there is still more to do. The United States will continue to work within the G20 and in other bilateral and multilateral engagements to promote and expand these policy pronouncements regarding responsible state behavior in cyberspace.

ORGANIZATION FOR SECURITY AND COOPERATION IN EUROPE

As a result of the leadership by the United States and like-minded countries, the 57 member states of the OSCE, which includes not only Western allies but also Russia and other former Soviet states, reached consensus in March 2016 on an expanded set of CBMs. This expanded set, which includes five new CBMs, builds upon the 11 CBMs announced by the OSCE in 2013 that member states are already working to implement.

The initial 11 CBMs were primarily focused on building transparency and putting in place mechanisms for de-escalating conflict. For example, there were CBMs calling upon participating states to identify points of contact that foreign governments could reach out to in the event of a cyber incident emanating from the state's territory and put in place consultation and mediation mechanisms. The additional five CBMs focused more on cooperative measures focusing on issues like cybersecurity of critical infrastructure and developing public-private partnerships. Secure and resilient critical infrastructure, including in the communications sector, requires the integration of cyber, physical, and human elements. Since most critical infrastructure is privately owned, public-private partnerships are essential for strengthening critical infrastructure. Given the distributed nature of critical infrastructure, these efforts also require international collaboration. Work will continue this year to strengthen implementation of the previous CBMs and to begin implementing the new ones as well. This will build on the cooperation we have underway with many international partners in this and other similar fora. We also hope that this further success within the OSCE context can serve to strengthen CBMs as a model that other regional security organizations can adopt.

In addition to our work with governmental organizations, the Department of State engages extensively with a range of stakeholders outside of government, who play critical roles in helping to preserve and promote the same vision of cyberspace held by the United States. Non-government stakeholders are often part of our delegations to key meetings, for which there is intensive consultation, and we often engage with our stakeholders before and after key events to hear their views and to inform them of our activities. We also engage extensively with the stakeholder community ahead of and immediately following major cyber conferences, such as the Global Conference on Cyberspace, most recently in The Hague, the Netherlands, and previously in Seoul, South Korea.

POLICY CHALLENGE: ALTERNATIVE VIEWS OF THE INTERNET

A challenge to the implementation of our cyberspace strategy is a competing and alternative view of the Internet. The United States and much of the broader international community support the open flow and movement of data on the Internet that drives economic growth, protects human rights, and promotes innovation. The United States believes in a multistakeholder approach whereby governments, private sector, civil society, and the technical and academic communities cooperate to address both technical and policy threats through inclusive, transparent, consensus-driven processes.

China's approach to cyberspace in the international context is propelled by its desire to maintain internal stability, maintain sovereignty over its domestic cyberspace, and combat what it argues is an emerging cyber arms race and 'militarization' of cyberspace. China has been willing to consider cyber confidence building measures, and has affirmed that international law applies in cyberspace, but has not been willing to affirm more specifically the applicability of the law of armed conflict or other laws of war, because it believes it would only serve to legitimize state use of cyber tools as weapons of war.

This has led to a set of external policies that reinforces traditional Chinese foreign policy priorities of non-interference in internal affairs, national sovereignty over cyberspace, and "no first use" of weapons. China views its expansive online censorship regime—including technologies such as the Great Firewall—as a necessary defense against destabilizing domestic and foreign influences, and it has promoted this conception internationally. China also urges creation of new "cyber governance" instruments, which would, inter alia, create new binding rules designed to limit the development, deployment, and use of "information weapons," promote speech and content controls, seek to replace the framework of the Council of Europe Convention on Cybercrime (Budapest Convention), elevate the role of governments vis-à-vis other stakeholders, and likely give the United Nations authority for determining attribution and responding to malicious cyber activity. While the United States and its partners seek to focus our cyber policy efforts on combatting threats to networks, cyber infrastructure, and other physical threats from cyber tools, China also emphasizes the threats posed by online content. In addition, some of these policies stand in sharp contrast to the U.S. view that all stakeholders should be able to contribute to the making of public policy regarding the Internet.

Russia's approach to cyberspace in the international context has focused on the maintenance of internal stability, as well as sovereignty over its "information space." While Russia co-authored the Code of Conduct, with China and other Shanghai Cooperation Organization members, Russia's ultimate goal is also a new international cyber convention, which they pair with criticism of the Budapest Convention.

Russia has nonetheless found common ground with the United States on our approach of promoting the applicability of international law to state conduct in cyberspace as well as voluntary, non-binding norms of state behavior in peacetime. Russia has also committed to the first ever set of bilateral cyber confidence building measures with the United States, as well as the first ever set of cyber CBMs within a multilateral institution, at the OSCE in 2013 and 2016 that I previously discussed.

We counter these alternative concepts of cyberspace policy through a range of diplomatic tools that include not only engagement in multilateral venues, but also direct bilateral engagement and awareness-raising with a variety of state and non-state actors. I now would like to discuss some of the technical challenges and threats the U.S. faces and some of the tools we have to respond to and prevent cyber incidents.

RESPONDING TO AND PREVENTING CYBER INCIDENTS

CONTINUING CYBER THREATS

Cyber threats to U.S. national and economic security are increasing in frequency, scale, sophistication, and severity. In 2015, high profile cyber incidents included the breach of health insurance company Anthem, Inc.'s IT system that resulted in the theft of account information for millions of customers; an unauthorized breach of the Office of Personnel Management's systems that resulted in the theft of approximately 22 million personnel files; and hackers launching an unprecedented attack on the Ukraine power grid that cut power to hundreds of thousands of customers.

Overall, the unclassified information and communications technology networks that support U.S. government, military, commercial, and social activities remain vulnerable to espionage and disruption. As the Department noted in the Strategy we submitted last month, however, the likelihood of a catastrophic attack against the United States from any particular actor is remote at this time. The Intelligence Community instead foresees an ongoing series of low-to-moderate level cyber operations from a variety of sources, which will impose cumulative costs on U.S. economic competitiveness and national security, pose risks to Federal and private sector infrastructure in the United States, infringe upon the rights of U.S. intellectual property holders, and violate the privacy of U.S. citizens.

In February, Director of National Intelligence James Clapper testified before Congress on the 2016 Worldwide Threat Assessment of the U.S. Intelligence Community, and stated: "Many actors remain undeterred from conducting reconnaissance, espionage, and even attacks in cyberspace because of the relatively low costs of entry, the perceived payoff, and the lack of significant consequences." He highlighted the malicious cyber activities of the leading state actors, non-state actors such as Da'esh, and criminals who are developing and using sophisticated cyber tools, including ransomware for extortion and malware to target government networks.

The Intelligence Community continues to witness an increase in the scale and scope of reporting on malicious cyber activity that can be measured by the amount of corporate data stolen or deleted, personally identifiable information compromised, or remediation costs incurred by U.S. victims. The motivation to conduct cyber attacks and cyber espionage will probably remain strong because of the gains for the perpetrators.

TOOLS AVAILABLE TO COUNTER CYBER THREATS

The United States works to counter technical challenges through a whole-of-government approach that brings to bear its full range of instruments of national power and corresponding policy tools—diplomatic, law enforcement, economic, military, and intelligence—as appropriate and consistent with applicable law.

The United States believes that deterrence in cyberspace is best accomplished through a combination of "deterrence by denial"—reducing the incentive of potential adversaries to use cyber capabilities against the United States by persuading them that the United States can deny their objectives—and "deterrence through cost imposition"—threatening or carrying out actions to inflict penalties and costs against adversaries that conduct malicious cyber activity against the United States. It is important to note that there is no one-size-fits-all approach to deterring or responding to cyber threats. Rather, the individual characteristics of a particular threat determine the tools that would most appropriately be used.

The President has at his disposal a number of tools to carry out deterrence by denial. These include a range of policies, regulations, and voluntary standards aimed at increasing the security and resiliency of U.S. government and private sector computer systems. They also include incident response capabilities and certain law enforcement authorities.

With respect to cost imposition, the President is able to draw on a range of response options from across the United States government.

Diplomatic tools provide a way to communicate to adversaries when their actions are unacceptable and to build support and greater cooperation among, or seek assistance from, allies and like-minded countries to address shared threats. Diplomatic démarches to both friendly and potentially hostile states have become a regular component of the United States' response to major international cyber incidents. In the longer term, U.S. efforts to promote principles of responsible state behavior in cyberspace, including peacetime norms, are intended to build increasing consensus among like-minded states that can form a basis for cooperative responses to irresponsible state actions.

Law enforcement tools can be used to investigate crimes and prosecute malicious cyber actors both within the United States and abroad. International cooperation is critical to cybercrime investigations, which is why the United States has promoted international harmonization of substantive and procedural cybercrime laws through the Budapest Convention, created an informal channel for data preservation and information sharing through the G7 24/7 network, and promoted donor partnerships to assist developing nations.

Economic tools, such as financial sanctions, may be used as a part of the broader U.S. strategy to change, constrain, and stigmatize the behavior of malicious actors in cyberspace. Since January 2015, the President has provided guidance to the Secretary of the Treasury to impose sanctions to counter North Korea's malicious cyber-enabled activities. Executive Order 13687 was issued, in part, in response to the provocative and destructive attack on Sony Pictures Entertainment, while Executive Order 13722 targets, among others, significant activities by North Korea to undermine cybersecurity, in line with the recently-signed North Korea Sanctions and Policy Enhancement Act of 2016. Aside from these North Korea-specific authorities, in April 2015, the President issued Executive Order 13694, Blocking the Property of Certain Persons Engaging in Significant Malicious Cyber-Enabled Activities, which authorizes the imposition of sanctions against persons whose malicious cyber-enabled activities could pose a significant threat to the national security, foreign policy, or economic health or financial stability of the United States.

Military capabilities provide an important set of options for deterring and responding to malicious cyber activity. The Department of Defense continues to build its cyber capabilities and strengthen its cyber defense and deterrence posture. As part of this effort, the Department of Defense is building its Cyber Mission Force, which is already employing its capabilities to defend Department of Defense networks, defend the Nation against cyberattacks of significant consequence, and generate integrated cyberspace effects in support of operational plans and contingency operations. In addition, Secretary of Defense Ashton Carter announced earlier this year that U.S. forces are using cyber tools to disrupt Da'esh's command and control systems and to negatively impact its networks.

Intelligence capabilities are also an important tool at the President's disposal in detecting, responding to, and deterring malicious activities in cyberspace, particularly given the unique challenges associated with attributing and understanding the motivation behind such malicious activities.

Even with this broad range of tools, deterring cyber threats remains a challenge. Given the unique characteristics of cyberspace, the United States continues to work to develop additional and appropriate consequences that it can impose on malicious cyber actors.

CAPACITY BUILDING

In addition to the tools that I have just outlined, the ability of the United States to respond to foreign cyber threats and fight transnational cybercrime is greatly enhanced by the capabilities and strength of our international partners in this area. Therefore, the Department of State is working with departments and agencies, allies and multilateral partners to build the capacity of foreign governments, particularly in developing countries, to secure their own networks as well as investigate and prosecute cybercriminals within their borders. The Department also actively promotes donor cooperation, including bilateral and multilateral participation in joint cyber capacity building initiatives.

In 2015, for example, the United States joined the Netherlands in founding the Global Forum on Cyber Expertise, a global platform for countries, international organizations, and the private sector to exchange best practices and expertise on cyber capacity building. The United States partnered with Japan, Australia, Canada, the African Union Commission, and Symantec on four cybersecurity and cybercrime capacity building initiatives. The Department also provided assistance to the Council of Europe, the Organization of American States, and the United Nations Global Program on Cybercrime to enable delivery of capacity building assistance to developing nations. Many traditional bilateral law enforcement training programs increasingly include cyber elements, such as training investigators and prosecutors in the handling of electronic evidence. Much of our foreign law enforcement training on combating intellectual property crime focuses on digital theft.

In another example of capacity building, the Department of State, through its Bureau of International Narcotics and Law Enforcement Affairs, manages five International Law Enforcement Academies (ILEAs) worldwide, and one additional Regional Training Center. These six facilities provide law enforcement training and instruction to law enforcement officials from approximately 85 countries each year. The ILEA program includes a wide variety of cyber investigation training courses, from basic to advanced levels, taught by subject matter experts from the U.S. Secret Service and other agencies and policy-level discussions with senior criminal justice officials. This serves as a force multiplier to enhance the capabilities of the international law enforcement community to collaborate in the effort to fight cybercrime.

The Department of State is committed to continuing its capacity building initiatives as another effective way to counter international cyber threats and promote international cyber stability.

LOOKING AHEAD

Cybersecurity will continue to be a challenge for the United States when we take into consideration the rapidly expanding environment of global cyber threats, the increasing reliance on information technology and number of "smart devices," the reality that many developing nations are still in the early stages of their cyber maturity, and the ongoing and increasingly sophisticated use of information technology by terrorists and other criminals. Thus, the Department of State anticipates a continued increase and expansion of our cyber-focused diplomatic and capacity building efforts for the foreseeable future.

The Department will continue to spearhead the effort to promote international consensus that existing international law applies to state actions in cyberspace and build support for certain peacetime norms through assisting states in developing technical capabilities and relevant laws and policies, to ensure they are able to properly meet their commitments on norms of international cyber behavior.

The Department of State remains appreciative of this Subcommittee's continued support. Thank you for the opportunity to testify today. I am happy to answer your questions.

Senator GARDNER. Thank you, Mr. Painter.
I will begin with questions.

Obviously, over the past several years, since 2011 with the publication of the International Strategy for Cyberspace out of the White House, we have seen activities from Russia attacking critical infrastructure in Ukraine last December. We have seen reports of targeting of U.S. critical infrastructure by various actors. We have seen news reports of Iranian agents attempting to access a dam near New York City. We have seen North Korea develop cyber as an asymmetric tool to threaten its neighbors and the United States. And we continue to see other actions despite the conversations and negotiations that we have.

And so in light of all these attacks from Russia, China, Iran, or supposed attacks from these nations, does the 2011 International Strategy for Cyberspace accurately reflect the threats that we face today, and if not, what has changed in the 2011 cyberspace strategy and what needs to change?

Mr. PAINTER. So I think the 2011 strategy was, as you know, a high level document that talked about our goals in cyberspace. Those goals have not changed. But I do think that as we look at the various challenges we are facing in cyberspace, particularly by various threat actors around the world, we are going to continue to hone the way we implement those goals and achieve those goals.

The strategy that we submitted to Congress, pursuant to the requirement of the committee, talks about both some of the threat actors that we are seeing but also some of the tools we have in our tool set to mitigate those threats and go after those threats. And that is going to be a continuing conversation. It needs to be a continuing and flexible approach that we have that uses a lot of the tools in our national tool set, really all the tools we have.

One thing we said in our international strategy in 2011 is that we need to look at all the tools we have as a government, a whole-of-government approach that uses everything from our economic tools, our diplomatic tools, certainly what I do, our law enforcement tools, our other trade tools that we might have, and even military tools in appropriate circumstances after we have exhausted other remedies. So we have to look at all the various tools we have.

I would say—on some of the issues you raised, I do not think we have made complete attribution, but on some we have—we have been using a variety of those tools. Certainly in terms of the diplomatic tools, we have used the tools that diplomats use. We have used them both against the people we are unhappy with and been very clear about what our concerns are. I would argue that the U.S.-China agreement came about because this was raised consistently at a very high level of our government as a major area of friction that would affect not just cyber issues between our two countries, but really the whole of the relationship. And that was significant.

I think the fact that we had other tools, including the law enforcement tools that were used to indict PLA officers in that case or more recently the indictment of the Iranian actors for the denial of service attacks and the penetration of the dam as a significant use of those tools that sends a deterrent message, and that is important.

We have a sanctions regime for cyber. We also have, thanks to both of you, additional sanctions authority for North Korea. We used North Korean sanctions authority after North Korea's attacks of Sony a couple of years ago. So we have used those tools, but we certainly have those other tools in our tool set.

So we really do have a variety of different ways to go after that. But we have to understand this threat is going to continue and it is going to evolve, and we need to be ready to deal with that evolution and use again all the tools in partnership. So I have a role in this, but I work with all of my interagency colleagues to do this.

The other thing I would mention is that part of the issue is also talking to not just our allies but other countries about what threats are out there. When I testified last year, I mentioned that we were the first office of our kind and that now there are over 20 countries around the world that have offices like mine. And a number of additional ones are looking at it. Australia just recently announced their cybersecurity strategy, and they are creating an office like mine, for instance. So, more and more countries are doing that. And that is significant because it means that we can, at a White House level, at a State Department level, talk with other countries and, again, in a whole-of-government way about what threats we are facing and what we may be able to do collectively.

And the third thing I mentioned goes back to the norms, and this is a long-term game. So we talked about law enforcement tools. We talked about trade tools. We talked about other tools. The norms of conduct that we are trying to promote and get more and more countries to sign up for and accept create an environment where there are rules of the road, where there is an expectation of what is appropriate conduct in cyberspace. If you have countries who are acting outside of that expectation, the countries who agree can act together to work against those transgressors. Now, that will take a while to build. We have had tremendous progress over the last year, but I think we are on the right track.

Senator GARDNER. In your written testimony, you talk about the various tools, diplomatic tools, law enforcement tools, economic tools, military capabilities, and intelligence capabilities. Obviously, you have talked about a number of diplomatic tools that have been utilized, talked about law enforcement tools that have been used to investigate cyber crimes and the work in partnership with other nations to enlist them in this investigative effort.

I want to talk a little bit more about the economic tools. Could you talk a little bit about the financial sanctions and when a determination is made by State-Treasury to move forward on economic sanctions?

Mr. PAINTER. Senator, as you know, the President signed a couple of executive orders, one right after the North Korea Sony attacks that were broad sanctions that went after members of the North Korean Communist Party and people who supported them. Two was the cyber sanctions order which was really the first of its kind anywhere in the world that targeted specifically various kinds of very serious cyber conduct. And then third, most recently, the North Korea Sanctions Act. And there is an EO now that gives voice to that last act, as well as U.N. Security Council resolutions.

That first sanctions order against North Korea has been used. The President, at the end, decides whether sanctions are used, and it is the right tool.

I would emphasize that is just one tool in the tool set. So if you look at the various tools, you will make a decision of what tools are appropriate in what case, and that can be flexible depending on the various threats you face. To date, the cyber sanctions order has not been used, but I am fully confident it will be used. I would also say the fact that it exists has a deterrent effect in and of itself and also changes behavior.

Senator GARDNER. You are referring to Executive Order 13694. Correct?

Mr. PAINTER. Correct.

Senator GARDNER. Is there any active consideration right now of sanctions under the executive order?

Mr. PAINTER. All I can say is that there is an interagency group that looks at this. It includes State. It includes Treasury, the White House, and it includes other agencies as well. I cannot make any statement about actual designations under that, but as I said, this is an important tool in our tool set and one I am confident will be used.

Senator GARDNER. Senator Cardin.

Senator CARDIN. Thank you again.

We are almost at the year anniversary of the announcement of the compromise by OPM of millions of Americans' information being compromised through a cyber attack. Millions of Federal workers are at risk today as a result of that attack. Their economic issues are very much at risk.

As a result of that announcement, I think it gave extra attention to the November agreement between the United States and China that we have referred to several times. Would the agreement we entered into with China be effective in preventing China from actively engaging in that type of attack against American Federal workers?

Mr. PAINTER. What I would say is that we obviously take that kind of activity very seriously. There has been a lot of work that the administration has done, including the one thing I did not mention in response to Senator Gardner's question, which is doing a lot of work to harden the targets, doing a lot of work to make sure we are doing deterrence by denial. So the recent CNAP announcements by the administration, both in terms of funding but also in terms of the programmatic changes to make sure that there is better protection of government systems, are part of how we keep that from happening in the future.

We have not made any public attribution of the OPM attack, as I believe you know, or the character of it. But what I would say is what we did say to China at the time—and I think Deputy Secretary Blinken mentioned this—is that kind of intrusion is just too big to ignore and too disruptive and it is a real concern.

With respect to the agreement that was made in the context of the Xi visit, there is agreement not to use cyber to steal intellectual property for purposes of benefiting a commercial sector. That was something we do not do. We do not think any country around the world should do. And quite frankly, as you know, China was not willing to make that distinction, the distinction between intelligence gathering that every country does and the kind of commercial theft and benefit——

Senator CARDIN. I think I know where your answer is leading, which is, no, it would not cover that type of a——

Mr. PAINTER. The other thing it did was create a number of mechanisms, including the mechanism that is led by the Attorney General and the Secretary of Homeland Security and the group that I lead that allows for messaging in those contexts where we did not have those messaging channels before.

Senator CARDIN. Well, here is why I think it does cover that. China's largest companies are government-owned. So how do you deal with the issue of competitive advantage to companies' commercial sectors when you are dealing with a country, China, where so much of its economy is controlled by the government? Does not their attack against our workforce very much affect their commercial advantage?

Mr. PAINTER. Specifically, what the agreement, which then got approved at the G20, is an agreement that was approved right after President Xi was here for his summit with President Obama—he went to U.K. Prime Minister Cameron and asked for a similar agreement. German Chancellor Angela Merkel asked for a similar agreement, and then we had the G20 statement. It specifically talks about theft of trade secrets, intellectual property as the thing that is being stolen to benefit a commercial sector. And even if it is a state-owned enterprise, I would submit that theft of intellectual property can be, even if it is going to a state-owned enterprise, violate that agreement if it is being used to benefit what is there in a commercial sector. So that is what we are working on. That is what we are looking at very closely.

Of course, we want to stop all kinds of intrusions. Of course, we want to stop intrusions even if they are for intelligence purposes. But we need to do as good a job as we can to make sure we are preventing those, and that is why the deterrence by denial and far better protection of our Federal networks is really important.

Senator CARDIN. Are you prepared to advise this committee as to whether the agreement with China has resulted in a reduced amount of activity by China in its attempts to steal intellectual property from American companies?

Mr. PAINTER. So the way I characterize this is—I think recently Admiral Rogers testified not to this committee but another committee—that we are watching very closely and the jury is still out. I think Director Comey said that he has seen some more cooperation on cyber crime cases. We are looking closely, and we are going to continue to look closely. And all of our government and all the tools of our government are being used to make sure that that commitment is being honored.

I would also make clear, however, that as the President said, words are not enough. We need to make sure that actions are matching and that we have not taken any tools off the table. We have not taken any of the tools we have, any of the tools I talked about in response to Senator Gardner's question, off the table if we find that China is not complying with the agreement.

Senator CARDIN. Well, I would just point out I support moving forward with protocols of other countries. You are dealing with a controlled economy. You are dealing with a communist country in China. And if the agreement does not protect our Federal workforce, then we can expect more in direct agreements with other countries. You do not invade the privacy of a workforce and call that intelligence gathering for your national security. That should be in the same category as the agreement that covers the theft of intellectual property. And if you are dealing with a country that has controlled companies, then we need to also understand that that needs to cover the type of activities that are being done by the Chinese Government.

So I hear what you are saying. And the Federal workforce very much depends upon the use of technology to protect them, but they also expect that we are going to be raising these issues at the highest levels in order to protect our workforce because they should not be fair game in the world of cyber activities.

Mr. PAINTER. I do not disagree. I am a member of the Federal workforce. So I totally agree.

Senator CARDIN. I am sure that there is an entity that now has all your personal information controlled by another country.

Mr. PAINTER. I think we need to do whatever we can to protect that information. I do think that you have seen a lot of activity, and it has really been sustained activity, but some of the recent announcements that talk about, for instance, appointing a White House CISO, Chief Information Security Officer—we have not had that before—trying to make sure we have much better protections including the DHS Einstein System—these are all critical, and this is not easy. You mentioned this is not easy because it is an asymmetric often, and making sure that you get the protections in place—it is hard to protect systems. But there is a lot of work we can and should be doing and we are.

Senator CARDIN. I have other questions, but I will wait until the next round.

Senator GARDNER. Thanks, Senator Cardin.

Just following up on the OPM question, in mid-March, Director Comey had a visit with some high level Chinese officials on further cyber crime issues, investigations. Do you know the subject matter of that conversation? Did it lead to OPM? Were there discussions about cooperation on finalizing or getting resolution of the OPM?

Mr. PAINTER. I will defer to the FBI for any substance of any conversations in law enforcement channels or investigatory channels. So I have no real comment on that.

Clearly one of the mechanisms that was set up was this mechanism that is led by the Attorney General and the Secretary of Homeland Security. There are a number of things that came out of that, including a protocol for making sure we are both sharing and making requests of information from each other, but I am not going to comment on any specific conversation that DOJ was involved in.

Senator GARDNER. When talking about the tools available, diplomatic tools, law enforcement tools, economic tools, and denial efforts and deterrence, the State Department is in communication with the Department of Defense on a number of these issues. Has the State Department ever denied a request by the Department of Defense for action in either retaliation or any other cyber actions that we should take?

Mr. PAINTER. There are a number of ways that we talk to the Department of Defense, and we as a government look at all these various policy issues. And we have been very supportive of the Department of Defense's strategies for operating in cyberspace. They now have two of them out. I have worked with them on those documents. I have a call every 2 weeks with my counterpart at DOD, at the OSD Policy where we talk about issues that are coming——

Senator GARDNER. And who do you consider your counterpart to be?

Mr. PAINTER. Aaron Hughes, who is the DASD for cyber, essentially for cyber over there, and before that it was Eric Rosenbach, who is now the Chief of Staff to the Secretary.

So we have very close coordination.

One of the things I do in my own Department is we have a monthly coordination group—in fact, we are meeting this afternoon—where we bring all the different agencies, including DOD, and all the different parts of the Department together to discuss our international engagement strategy. And then the White House holds a number of meetings at an IPC, interagency policy committee, level, at a CRG, which I will talk about in a moment, and also a deputies and principals level. So there is a lot of interaction.

I am not going to comment on specific operations or how those various things are considered. But I think one thing we are doing as a government that is first—and I mentioned in our strategy one of the tools we have seen is DOD developing its capabilities, having more mission teams that are dealing with this. And that is important. That is one part of deterrence. It is one part of our approach.

So there has been much more activity. There is much more unity of purpose. There is much more discussion of this. Our doctrine allows us to take all the different aspects into account, both what aspects we need to go after wrongdoers but also what the effects are on our foreign policy, what the effects are on other issues that we need to look at. Our policy, as I think you know, is to look at law enforcement and network security aspects, when we are talking about cyber defense, before going to other tools. Also certainly DOD is looking at tools in areas of hostility like ISIL. So that is another issue that we have been working on, but I cannot really get into those particular conversations.

Senator GARDNER. Without getting into the specifics of any kind of action, though, has the State Department said no to any——

Mr. PAINTER. Again, I am not going to comment on the discussions. I think there are continuing discussions, as there should be, on any possible operation that we do. And that is the same for any of the other tools.

Senator GARDNER. Let me rephrase the question then I guess. Are you in a position to say no to a Department of Defense strategy?

Mr. PAINTER. We have an interagency process. Just like DOD comments on our strategies and indeed commented on the strategy that I sent to you, we comment on strategies and things that they are doing as well. So it really is a whole-of-government process. This is not any one agency acting on their own. We are working as a team.

Senator GARDNER. Okay. For instance, North Korea. If the Department of Defense decided to take an action against North Korea because of a Sony attack or against Iran because of critical infrastructure, that discussion would go to the State Department. Correct?

Mr. PAINTER. That discussion would involve the State Department, but essentially it goes to the President. The President is the one who makes the decisions about what tools we use and what kinds of tools and when we use those tools.

Senator GARDNER. Who else at the White House is involved in that type of a decision on——

Mr. PAINTER. There is, just like there is in other areas, an interagency. There is a CRG, the cyber response group, of which State is a member. That is essentially an IPC level discussion. Discussions, depending on a particular topic, can go to a deputy's level, can go to a principal's level, and ultimately the President. It involves the National Security Advisor. It involves Lisa Monaco and others. It involves a range of different people as we look at all these really important policy issues.

This, Senator Gardner, is something that I personally have seen—I have been doing various aspects for 26 years. I have seen a real change over the last 5 or 6 years where we do have a good process that comes together to make sure we are looking at all the different aspects of this. Now, this is not unique to cyber, to be sure. But I think this is one of the ways it is done.

Senator GARDNER. You mentioned earlier in your testimony that your office is the first office of its kind and that many other nations now—I think you said 20 other nations—are creating some sort of office—a similar office. During the discussion and debate on the National Defense Authorization Act, there will be an amendment to create basically a cyber COCOM, a COCOM level cyber command, combatant command level. Do you believe that we should create any higher level cyber department, administration? Do you believe your position within the State Department should be elevated to perhaps special envoy level, ambassador level so that we can fully focus on this? Because this is an issue that is gaining in strategic importance and is going to be with us throughout our coming lives. And so are we focused enough on this and elevating it enough to the level of importance that it deserves?

Mr. PAINTER. I think we absolutely are. I report directly to the Secretary. I am in the Secretary's Office. The reason the office was created in the Secretary's Office was so that it could reach across the Department in really a very collaborative way and work with everyone from, as Senator Cardin was talking about, our democracy and human rights people on issues around Internet freedom, our Economic Bureau people on some of the economic and access issues and governance issues, our Counterterrorism Bureau and terrorist use of the Internet, our INL Bureau and some of the capacity building around law enforcement issues, AVC, arms control and verification.

We set the architecture up so that we can work with all these groups. And, as I mentioned, our monthly coordination group has done that.

I have not had any issue, I can say, in meeting with other counterparts around the world at any level in foreign ministries. I have not had any issue with our structure in making sure we can really aggressively go after the things we are trying to do. Look, I am a former prosecutor, so I am an impatient person as a rule. But the fact that we were able in the last year to do as we have done on something where just a year ago—just a year ago, I was sitting here and I was telling you about these norms of behavior. That is when they first got some publicity when I was telling you about it. And a year later, we have all this activity. That is significant. So neither the Department nor I personally really feel that we need to change it.

What I would say is I want to make sure that whoever comes in in the next administration—and I think this will happen at both the presidential level and the secretary level—continues to really see this as a priority area. As a coordinator, I am one of the special envoys, if you will. I am one of the people who looks across the Department and works with the Department to make sure we are elevating this issue, which did not really even exist as an issue area 5 years ago.

Senator GARDNER. But in terms of its own bureau, you do not think——

Mr. PAINTER. So here is the problem with its own bureau, and this is something that has been raised before. If you think about the crosscutting nature of this issue—and Senator Cardin, you mentioned this as well—when you are talking about everything from human rights and the importance of human rights, cybersecurity, cyber crime, international security, Internet governance, capacity building, if you create a bureau, you do two things.

One, you stovepipe it so that other people will say, well, that is a boutique issue. You guys go and deal with that.

Two, you would pull the people out of all the bureaus that need to do this. We are trying to mainstream this issue at the State Department. We are trying to make this something that is like every other foreign policy issue. We want people to deal with this in every bureau, regional bureau, and functional bureau. If you create a bureau, you have to pull the people out, and frankly they have to replicate it anyway. So that is not very effective.

We have not seen that being done in other countries around the world. They have the same sort of coordination function that they pursue.

I think that that actually is counterproductive to us making progress in this area because it is, by its nature, a distributed issue.

I would say one other thing. To give you an example of some of the things we have done, we just a couple of weeks ago—and I think I mentioned this to you when I saw you both recently—had a training for essentially our cyber diplomats. From over 100 posts around the world, we brought back the folks in those embassies who are charged with this issue. We are looking at this crosscutting issue. We have told each of them in the embassies to build a crosscutting team, get the political cone, get the economic cone, get the LEGAT if there is one, get the defense attache, get the whole group in the embassy to have a mini-team on this. That is really the model we are trying to promote.

Senator GARDNER. Thank you.

Senator Cardin.

Senator CARDIN. Thank you for mentioning human rights. Human rights, I have been told by the leaders in the Obama administration, is one of the Obama administration's top priorities for advancing not just American ideals but our national security because it very much affects the stability of regimes and prevents the voids from being created that adds to radicalization.

So let me just find out from you how active you are in promoting human rights in our cyber strategies. We have export control laws that deal with our weapon systems because we understand that American technology should not be used against America's national security. So, therefore, we restrict the ability of manufacturers to be able to export U.S. technology. They have to proceed under certain procedures.

American technology in the cyber area is the best in the world. What steps are we taking to make sure that American companies are not exporting technology in cyber that is being used by repressive regimes to violate the human rights of its citizens?

Mr. PAINTER. This is an issue we are very concerned about. We are certainly concerned about the use of these technologies. But as I think you also know, they are dual-use technologies. We are both concerned about technologies that could be used by repressive regimes to monitor citizens, but we are also worried about tools that could be used by regimes that are not our friends to attack us. So we do not want to have either of those things happen. We want to make sure of that and we are committed to keeping the most dangerous cyber tools from the most dangerous actors.

At the same time, we are also committed to supporting the ability of our businesses, our consumers, and the government to defend themselves from cyber threats and to promote innovation in cybersecurity. So we have been talking a lot to our industry colleagues about this issue.

As I think you may know, there was an agreement in the so-called Wassenaar Group to create certain controls for cyber technology that could either be used, as you said, by repressive regimes for monitoring of its citizens or to attack us. We are and the Department of Commerce is in particular looking at how can they get that implemented. We are actually going back to Wassenaar, which has 40 participating states, to talk about how those might actually apply and whether we need to make some changes in those controls that were agreed to.

That is just one area of nonproliferation, but that is an important one. And we need to make sure that we are addressing this. And even as we talked at Wassenaar about making changes so we can promote innovation and cybersecurity while, at the same time, targeting the behavior you talk about, we need to do that in the right way.

Whatever will happen with Wassenaar in the negotiations there, we also, as we implement this, need to make sure we walk that line in an appropriate way. And we have been talking a lot and

Commerce has to our private sector, but we will also have at least another——

Senator CARDIN. You know that American companies today are using their technology to support repressive policies of other countries as a way of gaining entry into the markets of those countries. Are we trying to develop policies that will prevent the use of American technology for the repressive actions of regimes against its own people?

Mr. PAINTER. As I said, I think the one area where we have done this is in this Wassenaar area, but it is a very delicate balance to make sure we are not stifling either innovation or stifling cybersecurity. That is one area.

The other is my colleagues in DRL have been promoting—we have been promoting together—the idea of business responsibility and protection of fundamental human rights and how you have businesses look at that issue. And the thing that we have been promoting there in a couple different aspects—one is the Global Network Initiative, which is a group of businesses that looks at what the ethics are and what the rules are for businesses. And this is a voluntary association. A number of businesses are part of that.

The other is in the context of something called the Freedom Online Coalition, which I think I mentioned to you last year Tom Malinowski and I had just gone to the meeting, and we support that group very much. It is going to have the next meeting in Costa Rica, so in our region for the first time, coming up this year, which is significant because getting more of our region as part of that, that that is important.

I should also say that as we do these all-of-government dialogues that we do with multiple countries around the world now, human rights are always a part of that. So it is not just about cybersecurity. Human rights are a part of it. As we do capacity building, we weave that in too.

This Freedom Online Coalition has talked about some of the responsibilities of businesses, some of the tension between security and human rights, and that is a continuing discussion.

This is not an easy area, but we want to make sure, as I said, that the most dangerous tools are not given to the most dangerous actors while at the same time making sure we are protecting innovation.

Senator CARDIN. I would hope that you would be aggressive in developing protocols related to the use of technology, as well as some of the other areas that you are working on as it relates to protecting human rights.

I would also hope as you look at this delicate balance—and it is a delicate balance. I do not deny that. But I would hope that you will use the same sensitivities that we use for military arms as we use for Internet technology so that we are not wrapped up in the view that the Internet is so global that technology development in the United States must be immediately made available globally when it can be used by repressive regimes to trample on the human rights of its citizens.

I also think there has got to be a tradeoff with corporate responsibility, and there needs to be protocols which American businesses are prepared to adhere to and not just yield to the unreasonable demands of repressive regimes.

Let me ask one more question, if I might, Mr. Chairman, and that is can you tell me or do you intend to clarify when an attack on cyber would trigger an inherent right of self-defense pursuant to article 51 of the U.N. Charter. When do we get to that point?

Mr. PAINTER. So a couple things. I do not think we have actually defined that with exceptional clarity in the physical world either. And there is a reason for that. Because it is often dependent on the circumstances of the attack.

However, there is nothing magic about cyber.

Senator CARDIN. When you say that—and I understand the sensitivities here again, but if it is not clear, then countries can try to test and test and test and pull us to the line and say they did not know that that would trigger the military response on self-defense. So to me clarity is important here.

Mr. PAINTER. As I said, we do not do this in the physical world. There is a reason, not just the fact it is a factual basis. But if you create clear red lines——

Senator CARDIN. Which we do on physical invasion of a NATO ally. That is a clear red line.

Mr. PAINTER. But in cyberspace, as you create some clear red lines, you give an incentive to actors to creep up to that red line knowing that they do not risk retaliation or do not risk response, and that does not create a good environment either. So you do need—and I think the deterrent strategy that was submitted by the Department of Defense recently talked about the need for— some strategic ambiguity here, which is important.

Now, we have said—and one of the things we got agreement with both in the context of this recent GGE—is article 51 actually does apply to cyberspace, and that there is activity. And that activity could be looked at just like you look at physical activity. Is it causing death and serious injury? Is it causing major damage? Those are the kind of factors that are used now to look at physical space. Use the same factors in cyberspace. You do not use a different set of factors. And so that is one of the things we are pursuing.

And then one of the other issues is, as you know, we continue to make sure that cyber is part of NATO's core operating precepts, and we have said that article 5 in NATO could apply in a cyber incident. It is going to be a case-by-case basis, but we are going to look at all those factors as well.

I should also just mention, to Senator Gardner's question about the bureau, the issues you raise with respect to human rights is another reason why when my office was created, the point was to not just look at the security issues, but to draw in all these other interests and make sure that our approach both upheld human rights and looked at the security issues. It is important to have those together.

Senator CARDIN. I just would underscore this point. I do not follow your point on article 51, and I will say the reasons why.

When you are talking about conventional threats, you know when those conventional threats have been initiated, and you know the consequences if you do not defend yourself from those attacks. In cyber, we are being attacked every second, and to a large extent, the consequences depend upon the success of the cyber attacks. And we may not know about the cyber attacks, as in the OPM hack. We did not know about it until well after they had penetrated and gotten the information, which puts millions of Americans at risk. At risk.

I understand you want to use conventional standards for whether our security has been compromised from the point of view of public safety, et cetera. But in cyber you just do not have the luxury of knowing that until maybe it is too late. So, therefore, a country will say we will take it to the point until we get discovered, and then we will say, gee, we did not mean to do it. And therefore, there is no response under article 51.

Mr. PAINTER. But there is no limitation that we cannot take a range of different actions. The whole idea of having all these different tools that we talked about in our toolkit is that we can take those actions, even if it does not reach the level of an article 51 armed attack. An armed attack is a specific term that triggers the right to self-defense in a particular way. And even when that threshold is reached, we sometimes as a country might decide not to respond.

Senator CARDIN. I understand. The military is the last resort always.

Mr. PAINTER. Right. So we can still use all these tools we have.

And I would also say there is a difference, and I think the DNI talked about this recently—or not that recently, but fairly recently. There is a difference between an attack and an intrusion. An attack, a destructive attack, is different than an intrusion and the kind of disruptive effects it has under international law. One of the things we have been pioneering this idea as part of our framework that international law applies in cyberspace. That was not clear a couple years ago. It was seen as a free fire zone. International law means there are rules, including the triggering of article 51, including proportionality and distinction when you actually have a shooting war. All those things are important, and we need to look at all the tools we have even if it is below that threshold.

The idea behind the norms I talked about, not attacking the critical infrastructure of another country absent wartime, is that gives us some rules of the road even when you do not reach that high level because that is the activity we see every day. We do not see armed conflict every day. We see the theft of intellectual property. We see potential attacks against infrastructure. We see attacks against CERTs. Those are the rules of the road we are trying to promote so that we have activities we can do even below that high threshold.

Senator CARDIN. Thank you.

Senator GARDNER. Thank you, Senator Cardin.

Mr. Painter, just to follow up on a few of those questions.

On critical infrastructure in particular, do you think that Russia's attacks against Ukraine's power grid in 2015, December, violated its commitment to the United Nations on critical infrastructure?

Mr. PAINTER. As I believe you know, we have not made any attribution of that incident. We are very concerned about that kind of attack and that kind of incident, and we have characterized that as an attack. We had an interagency group at DHS and DOE and others work with the Ukrainians in the aftermath of that. So it is something of concern.

One of the things that we have done is—not me personally but our DHS colleagues—also made warnings to our own electrical grid and made sure that they were aware of what the risks were of this kind of attack. It is something we take very seriously.

But we have not attributed that. I am not going to attribute it. I am not going to characterize what it is.

Senator GARDNER. Do you believe that Russia is still attempting to penetrate U.S. critical infrastructure?

Mr. PAINTER. I would defer to what the DNI said in terms of Russia, China, Iran, and North Korea being the major threat actors we are seeing and that Russia has a full spectrum of activities. But in this setting, I will not——

Senator GARDNER. And so does that activity violate their commitment to the United Nations?

Mr. PAINTER. Again, I am not going to characterize what Russia is doing in this setting. However, if there is an attack, our view— and it is a voluntary norm. It is a voluntary norm at this point, which has been agreed to. But if there is an attack on critical infrastructure by another country, first of all, we are going to take it seriously whether there is a norm or not. We are going to be able to use all the tools we have in our toolkit.

Second, we do not want any country to do that, and it is exactly why we are promoting those norms around the world. If countries do do it, then we have to make sure we can work with other countries against those transgressors and also use the tools we have to defend ourselves.

Senator GARDNER. And so when we see penetration by Russia or Iran into critical infrastructure of the United States, whether that is an actual attack or whether that is preparing the battlefield, as it was characterized at one point, is that a violation of United Nations norms?

Mr. PAINTER. I think we are certainly concerned about those kinds of penetrations and those intrusions, and I think, as you know, in the case of Iran, there was an indictment from our Department of Justice against an actor not just for the denial of service attacks that we played a role in mitigating—I mentioned the last time we were here the State Department actually worked with other countries to ask them to mitigate the botnets all over the world—but also into the penetration of the dam and the SCADA system there. Those are really concerning issues, and we are going to make sure that we use the tools we have. In this case, there has been an indictment. There could be other tools in the future.

Senator GARDNER. Have you witnessed a change in behavior from Iran toward the United States in terms of cyber activities against the United States since the nuclear agreement of October 2015? Did you anticipate a change?

Mr. PAINTER. I would defer that question to the DNI who I think has addressed this in a more classified setting. I will say the DNI has continued to characterize Iran as one of the threat actors— Iran, North Korea, Russia, and China.

Senator GARDNER. Both before and after the nuclear agreement.

Mr. PAINTER. I think the DNI threat assessment was relatively recent.

Senator GARDNER. Your response to revelations—I think it was in the "New York Times"—regarding U.S. capabilities to significantly degrade or destroy Iran's nuclear capabilities before the JCPOA negotiations began. There was an article that talked about had they failed, there was a possible cyber exercise that could be taken against Iran to bring down their nuclear provisions. Were you a part of those discussions?

Mr. PAINTER. Again, I cannot comment on any operations or any plans that the United States may have had in this area, particularly——

Senator GARDNER. Was the State Department cyber office involved?

Mr. PAINTER. I would say more generally the State Department at some level was involved in all the decisions involving the use of cyber capabilities.

Senator GARDNER. Was the office of cyber——

Mr. PAINTER. Again, I cannot really get into that in this——

Senator GARDNER [continuing]. Because I just want to know whether or not you were a part of any discussions.

Mr. PAINTER [continuing]. Either our office or the State Department as a whole, depending on what the particular issue is, is involved in these discussions, as a policy matter all the time. And again, I cannot comment on that particular issue.

Senator GARDNER. And I am not trying to get you to give me any details of it, but I just want to make sure that I understand.

Mr. PAINTER. I am not going to even comment on whether that was actually a fact or whether that was being considered. I am not going to comment on that.

However, what I would say is the State Department is involved in discussions with respect to really all the tools we use as part of the interagency discussion. And one of the changes that I mentioned before is that I would say several years ago, the State Department had much more of a minor involvement in a lot the discussions, and now I think the discussions are—the State Department is one of the key players, as we discuss any of these issues.

Senator GARDNER. The cyber agreement that Senator Cardin spoke of earlier—how involved was the State Department in drafting that or your office in drafting the cyber agreement?

Mr. PAINTER. You mean with——

Senator GARDNER. The Chinese.

Mr. PAINTER [continuing]. Very, very involved. I think as you know, President Xi sent out his special envoy Meng Jianzhu to the United States about 10 days before the official visit. There were a number of meetings which I personally participated in and a meeting also that Secretary Kerry participated in. So we were very involved in that. And we were involved in the all-night negotiations that led to that agreement, and I personally was. So we were very involved in that.

Senator GARDNER. Senator Cardin?

The final questions I have—I know we are going to be voting here soon. Just in terms of China's activities, you mentioned it is premature to comment on whether the agreement has actually deterred the collection of commercial information for gain of its own commercial sector. We talked about Russia's possibility of attacks against Ukraine, whether or not that violates the agreements of the United Nations. We talked about Iran's activities and identifying China, Russia, Iran as ongoing challenges for the United States in cyber.

Is it time for a new framework of negotiation? We know Russia and China will not agree on what we believe should be secure cyberspace, open, free Internet. Is it time that we move forward with likeminded nations, the Five Eyes or the Ottawa Group, that we move forward in our own ideas with our own nations to create a block of interested parties that can then use that as leverage against others who simply are not going to behave the way they should——

Mr. PAINTER. Well, that is precisely what we are doing with these norms. Even though it is important to get China and Russia to agree to it as key countries—and that is what we have been doing—we have been trying to expand the likeminded tent, certainly with our Five Eyes allies but also with the EU and other countries in Europe, with countries in our own region. The whole idea of this expansion—and I mentioned one of the other things that has happened in the last year is that the President in almost every meeting with a foreign leader and every summit or when we have high level meetings with other governments on a diplomatic level has raised this issue of the importance of norms in cyberspace, the importance of this international security framework. To give you an example, Japan, India, China, Pakistan, the East Asian Summit, U.S.-EU at my level, Australia, ASEAN, the G7 Foreign Ministers meeting, and the GCC have all had statements. And most recently, just a couple weeks ago when the Nordic leaders were all here, there was a statement about cyber norms in there. So that is important to continue to advance that framework.

That is different than trying to have a cyber treaty. I think one of the concerns we have about the cyber treaty is that it is often advocated by the Chinese and Russians to try to control cyber weapons, as they say, but really they are trying to control—and this goes to Senator Cardin's point—they are trying to control information. They view information as destabilizing, and they talk about information security. That is not a productive path for us.

That is why the path that we have chosen, which I think is the most productive, is to promote how international law applies, norms in cyberspace, and confidence building measures among our likeminded, but make the likeminded tent bigger. That means working with the developing world as well, and a lot of the capacity building efforts are aimed that way.

Senator GARDNER. But do those agreements—I mean, that obviously does not include Russia or China.

Mr. PAINTER. Well, Russia and China have signed up to the agreements within the GGE, and they will be part of the——

Senator GARDNER. They continue to violate——

Mr. PAINTER. They continue to pose concerns, but so do other countries and other actors, including criminal and other actors, transnational organized groups around the world. So we need to promote and create expectations of what these agreements mean and what consequences there will be. That is part of the long-term effort, Senator. This is not an overnight development.

Senator GARDNER. So the model of likeminded nations, though, if we were to enter into some kind of agreement on this universal agreement areas—I mean, excluding them because obviously they are not going to——

Mr. PAINTER. I think it is important we are trying to promote international cyber stability. The reason I think there has been up-take on these norms is that Russia and China do not want their critical infrastructures attacked either. We want the widest possible group that is agreeing to those. And then we want to be able to act collectively against transgressors. We are not there yet. We have made tremendous progress in the last year, but as you know, part of our strategy going forward is getting more and more countries to sign up to it. For China to do some written agreement I just think is premature in this area. There is too much more we need to do to understand what the expectations are even with our close allies, and we are continuing to do that.

Senator GARDNER. But it is clear that—I mean, you would agree that neither China nor Russia has lived up to their agreements.

Mr. PAINTER. I would not say that. I would say this framework—international law, the norms in cyberspace, and confidence building measures—is increasing and will increase international stability. Yes, there will continue to be threat actors out there. Yes, countries around the world will continue to gather intelligence as countries have since the beginning of time. We need to do a better job and so do other countries in protecting ourselves against it. But China took off—the most destabilizing contact off the table and have mechanisms to discuss and raise with them—that is what the confidence building measures are about—are part of that way of addressing that.

Then, frankly, the backup to this is all the tools I talked about before. If countries are not abiding by that, to use all the tools, including diplomatic, which is my area, but also our law enforcement tools, our trade tools, the range of tools we have. We need to be ready and willing and continue to use those.

Senator GARDNER. Does the range of tools include things like the strategy to ban cyber weapons similar to like an NPT kind of thing?

Mr. PAINTER. Again, I do not know what a cyber weapon is. I think that the problem is we look at effects.

Senator GARDNER. But it is important that we do know what a cyber weapon is because that means——

Mr. PAINTER. Well, no.

Senator GARDNER [continuing]. Because different triggers under article 51 and others.

Mr. PAINTER. But no. A cyber weapon can be dual-use, and that is particularly true in the cyber arena. What we focused on, instead of cyber weapons, is we looked at effects. If you look at the norms we are talking about, it is what effects will they have, you know, attacking critical infrastructure. What is the endpoint, not what tool do you use, whether that is a dual-use tool or not. And so trying to restrict a quote/unquote cyber weapon I think, first of all, with changing technology is not going to work. And secondly, I think it would have an effect in terms of the dual-use technologies that are used to protect us.

Senator GARDNER. Is there any dual-use for malware or ransomware?

Mr. PAINTER. I think researchers will tell you that they use malware and antivirus companies and others to try to protect our systems and better understand the threats that are out there.

Senator GARDNER. It is sort of a Good Samaritan approach. Correct?

Mr. PAINTER. Well, I think you have to be careful in terms of what you are actually trying to control. This is exactly the issue that we have raised that we have run up into in the Wassenaar arrangement where we are trying to make sure we walk that balance where we are prohibiting governments from getting really bad tools that we do not want them to have, but at the same time, we are not inadvertently or advertently actually affecting industry's ability to protect itself with new and innovative tools.

Senator GARDNER. So you do not anticipate any kind of like a weapons of mass destruction type ban when it comes to cyber because you are concerned that we cannot define what a cyber weapon is.

Mr. PAINTER. What I would say, Senator, is I think the correct course is for us and not just our allies, but as large a community as we can muster, to pursue this idea of what effects we are trying to control, what are the rules of the road, what are the norms that we want, how does international law apply, how do we communicate with each other—and there has been a lot of good work there too—to make sure we have a long-term, stable environment in cyberspace. That is what we need to do. That is, I think, a more effective route especially now.

We are still in the beginning of this conversation. Yes, we had lots of progress since I talked to you last year, but you compare this to nuclear or others, we are really in the infancy of a lot of these conversations.

So I think that the path we are on is exactly the right path to raise awareness about these issues and what the threats are and to talk about what things that we are not going to do and we do not think anyone should do. I think that is more effective than going to some treaty.

Senator GARDNER. Final question. Senator Cardin, did you have anything that you wanted to ask?

Senator CARDIN. I am fine. Again, I thank Mr. Painter.

Senator GARDNER. Just one question. I mean, is there a discussion amongst nations to try to define what a cyber weapon is?

Mr. PAINTER. I think there have been discussions in the past and it has always run into some of the problems that I mentioned. With dual-use technology and new sorts of attacks and new technologies in place, it is difficult to say what a "cyber weapon" is, and I think more and more countries are looking at what are the effects we are trying to prohibit.

Senator GARDNER. But if we had some kind of an agreement amongst nations of what a cyber weapon is and defining they are dual-use but when used a certain way as a weapon, would that not help?

Mr. PAINTER. Again, I think it runs into all the problems that I just mentioned. It runs into all the problems in terms of how do you define it and that does cover inadvertently things that you need for research, things that you need to actually protect ourselves from some of the computer security companies. Again, I think the most effective way to address this is to go after what effects we are looking at, make sure that there are some clear understandings of what effects that we do not think countries should do, and that there are consequences for those effects.

Senator GARDNER. We have agreements on radioisotopes and other things that are dual-use. Why can we not do it with cyber?

Mr. PAINTER. I think it is much more complicated in this area than that. I think that these—first of all, radioisotopes are radioisotopes. These kinds of tools will continue to evolve and change and have different uses. So I do not think we can really freeze this in place.

Senator GARDNER. Thank you.

Senator Cardin, if no further questions, I want to thank you, Mr. Painter. I believe the vote has started. So thanks to everyone for attending today's hearing and to Mr. Painter for providing us with your testimony.

For the information of the members of the committee, the record will remain open until the close of business Friday, including for members to submit questions for the record. Mr. Painter, we would ask that you please promptly reply to any questions for the record as soon as possible, and they will be made a part of the record.

With the thanks of the committee, this hearing is now adjourned.

[Whereupon, at 11:10 a.m., the hearing was adjourned.]

○